INTRODUCTION

This book is a culmination of my childhood. Growing up in rural Pennsylvania I was very isolated. Fortunately I discovered origami and I gained the ability to make my own toys. The models in this book are developed from my experience with the art, and my knowledge of engineering and aerodynamics. Most of the models in this book require that you use foil paper, which can be purchased at your local arts and crafts store, or online. When folding the models, be sure to use the correct paper size, and to follow the instructions carefully. If you wish to fold models that are camouflage, simply print the design on a piece of computer paper, and tape it to your foil paper. If you wish for your models to be waterproof you can purchase some spray enamel, which is basically clear spray paint, and spray it on the paper before you fold it. Or, you can buy some spray adhesive, and laminate the paper with cellophane. Most of my jets work well with this type of paper, and I designed some of them using it. I have spent many hours with these models, and I hope you do as well.

TABLE OF CONTENTS

PHOTOGRAPHS OF THE MODELS
PAGE 4

SYMBOLS AND SIGNS
PAGE 7

PROCEDURES
PAGE 8

MISSILES

IMPALER

PAGE 10

JAVELIN

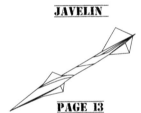

PAGE 13

HARPOON

PAGE 16

TANKS AND GROUND VEHICLES

THOR

PAGE 20

PREDATOR

PAGE 24

MARAUDER

PAGE 28

WARTHOG

PAGE 32

GUARDIAN

PAGE 36

JETS

WRAITH

PAGE 41

SPECTRE

PAGE 45

VIPER

PAGE 49

FALCON

PAGE 53

BRIMSTONE

PAGE 57

GRIFFON

PAGE 61

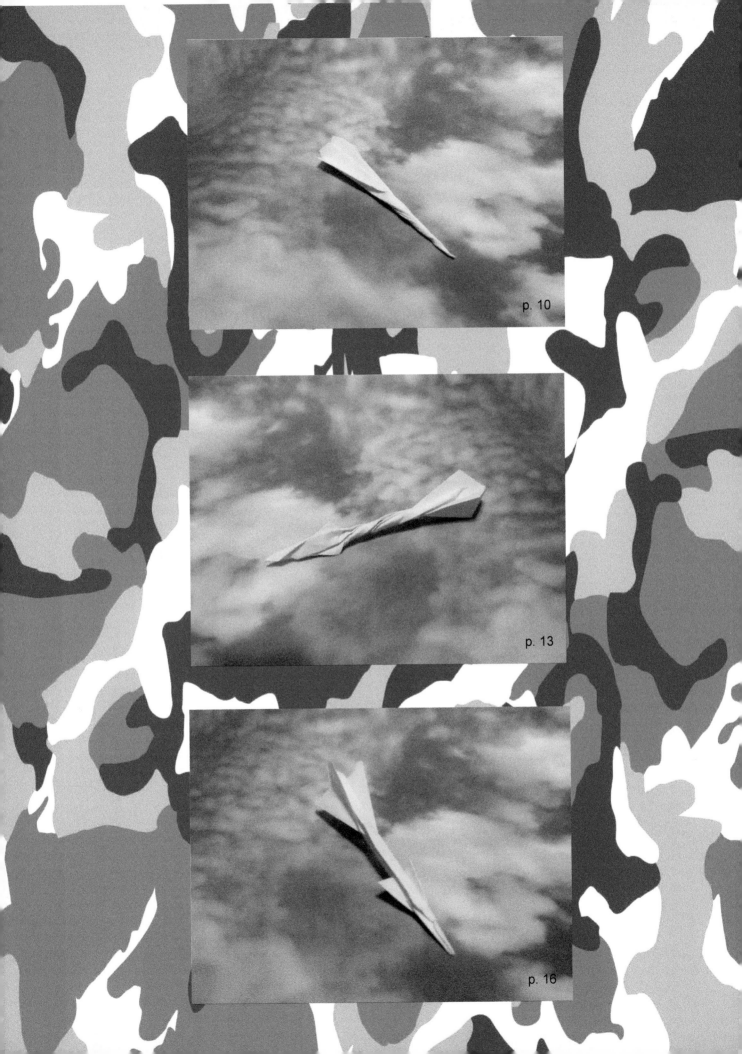

p. 10

p. 13

p. 16

p. 20

p. 24

p. 28

p. 32

p. 36

p. 41

p. 45

p. 49

p. 53

p. 57

p. 61

SYMBOLS AND SIGNS

Lines

_____ This line indicates an edge.

.... This line indicates a hidden edge.

- - - - - - - - - - This line indicates where to make a valley fold.

- · - · - · - · - · - This line indicates where to make a mountain fold.

.... This line indicates a hidden fold.

Arrows

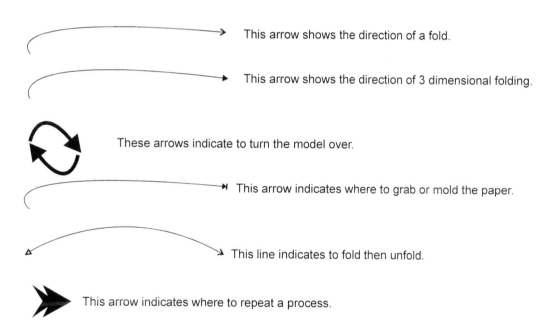

This arrow shows the direction of a fold.

This arrow shows the direction of 3 dimensional folding.

These arrows indicate to turn the model over.

This arrow indicates where to grab or mold the paper.

This line indicates to fold then unfold.

This arrow indicates where to repeat a process.

PROCEDURES

Inside reverse fold

1.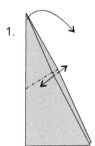

2.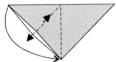

Partially open the sides out and push the top in.

Outside reverse fold

1.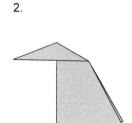

2.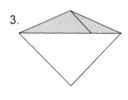

Partially open the sides out and push the top backward.

Squash fold

1.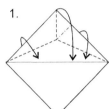

2.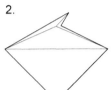

Pull the sides apart and push the corner down.

Rabbit ear fold

1.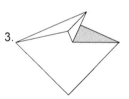

2.

3.

Push the two sides in and fold the corner over.

In progress.

Swivel fold

1.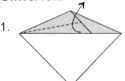

2.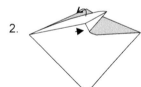

3.

Pull the top layer up.

Continue to pull the layer until it lies flat. Push the area that stands up down.

Petal fold

1.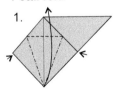

2.

3.

Pull the top layer up and push the sides in.

In progress.

Open sink

1.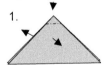

2.

3.

Push the top in and partially open the paper.

Continue to push the top and push the sides in.

Closed sink

1.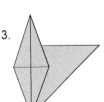

2.

3.

Push the top in while keeping the paper together.

In progress.

Preliminary fold

1.

2.

3.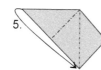
Squash fold the flap down.

4.
Turn the paper over.

5. Squash fold the flap down.

6.

Jet fold

1.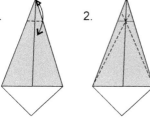

2.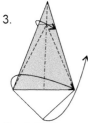
Fold then unfold the sides as shown.

3.
Push the lower part in and push the sides together using the creases you just made.

4. In progress.

5.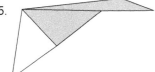

IMPALER MISSILE

You must use a square sheet of paper that is less than 3 x 3 in.

1.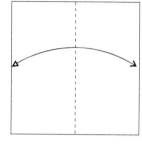

Fold the paper in half
then unfold it.

2.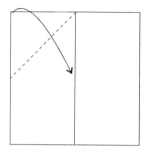

Valley fold the corner in
as shown. Then turn the
model over.

3.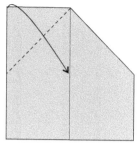

Valley fold the corner in
as shown.

4.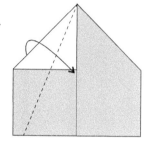

Fold the edge in as
shown. Then turn the
model over.

5.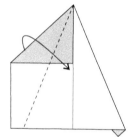

Valley fold the edge in
as shown.

6.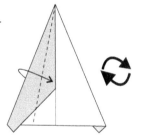

Fold the edge in as
shown. Then turn the
model over.

7.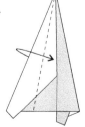

Fold the edge in as
shown.

8.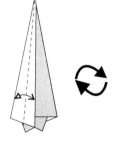

Fold then unfold as
shown. Then turn the
model over.

9.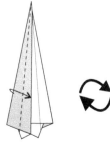

Fold the edge in as
shown. Then turn the
model over.

10.

Valley fold the edge in
as shown.

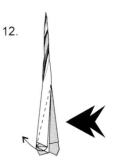

11.

Grab the area noted and twist
the end. The length will vary
depending on the size and
thickness of the paper used.

12.

Fold the small flap out a
little. Repeat behind.

13.

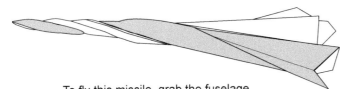

To fly this missile, grab the fuselage
just in front of the tailfins and throw
it as hard as you can. The harder
you throw it, the farther it will spin
and fly.

JAVELIN MISSILE

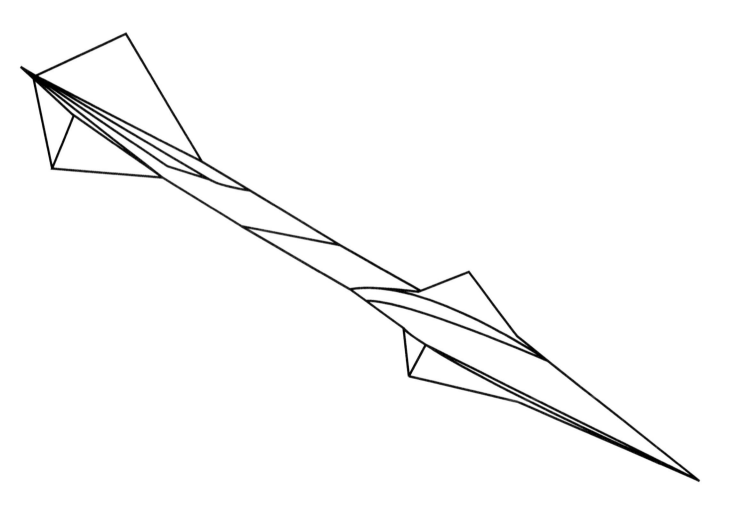

You must use a square sheet of paper no larger than 3 x 3 in. in order for this model to work.

1.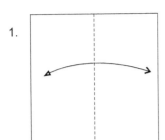

2.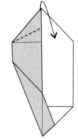

3.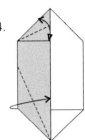

4.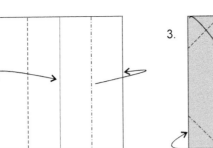

5.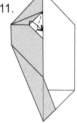

6.

7.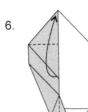

8.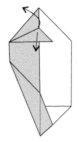

9.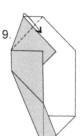

10.

Pull the trapped paper from the top of the flap down. Squash fold the bottom flap.

Swivel fold the paper out. Refer to step 9 as a guide.

11.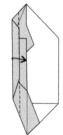

12.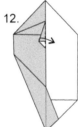

13.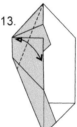

14.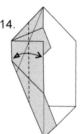

15.

16.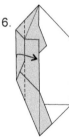

17.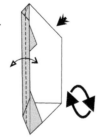

18.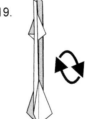

Fold the side in half, then unfold. Turn the model over then repeat steps 4–18 on the other side.

19.

Turn the model over.

20.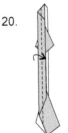

Fold on the existing crease.

21.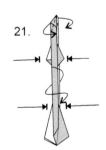

Round the point using the existing creases. Grab the sides shown and twist the model as far as it will go without tearing.

22.

Fold the tailfins perpendicular to each other.

23.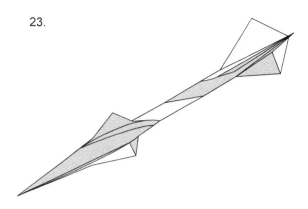

Throw the missile as hard as you can. It can fly up to 90 feet.

ATTACHING THE JAVELIN TO THE VIPER

1.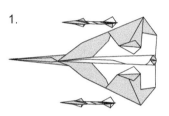

In order for the missiles to fit in the missile racks you must make a Viper (see page 49) from a square 8½ inches wide and two javelins from a 2¼ square.

2.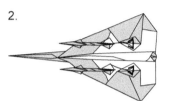

Take two perpendicular tailfins and slide them into the pockets shown.

3.

The jet can fly with the missiles attached. To fly the missiles, simply remove them again.

HARPOON
MISSILE

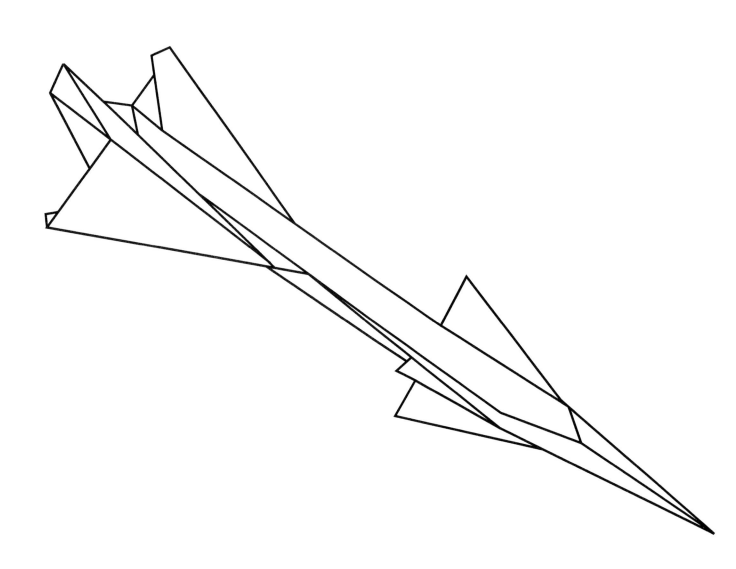

Use a square sheet of paper measuring 2–10 inches.

1.
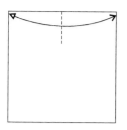

Fold the top corner to the other side, and unfold just the top part of the paper. Then turn the paper over.

2.
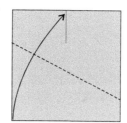

3.
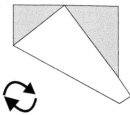

Turn the paper over.

4.
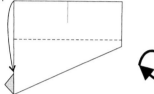

Fold the top corner down to the intersection shown. Then turn the paper over.

5.

6.
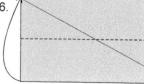

7.

Fold the paper down, then unfold it. Rotate the paper 90°. Refer to step 8.

8.
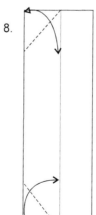

Fold then unfold the corners.

9.
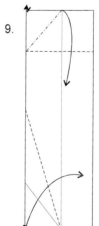

Fold then unfold the bottom corner, then squash fold the top corner.

10.
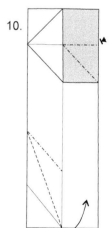

First, inside reverse fold the paper at the top. Then swivel fold the bottom edge out.

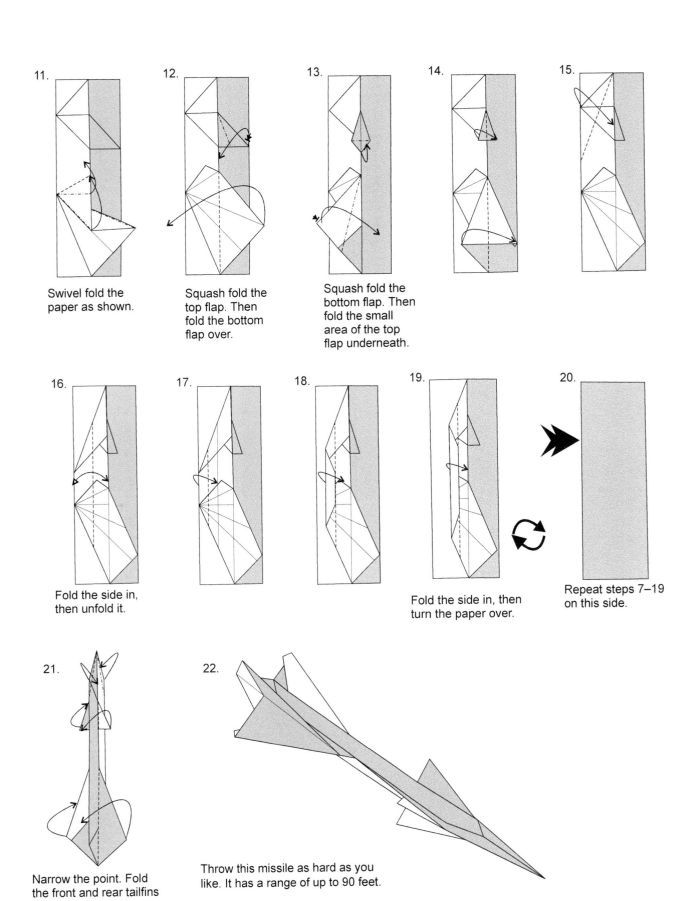

11.
Swivel fold the
paper as shown.

12.
Squash fold the
top flap. Then
fold the bottom
flap over.

13.
Squash fold the
bottom flap. Then
fold the small
area of the top
flap underneath.

14.

15.

16.
Fold the side in,
then unfold it.

17.

18.

19.
Fold the side in, then
turn the paper over.

20.
Repeat steps 7–19
on this side.

21.
Narrow the point. Fold
the front and rear tailfins
perpendicular to the
fuselage.

22.
Throw this missile as hard as you
like. It has a range of up to 90 feet.

ATTACHING THE HARPOON TO THE FALCON

1.

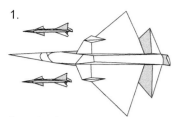

In order for the harpoon missiles to fit inside the missile racks, make a Falcon (see page 53) from an 8½ inch square, and two harpoons from two 2¼ inch squares.

2.

Take two perpendicular canard fins and slide them into the missile racks like shown.

3.

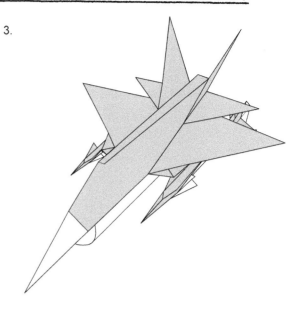

The jet can fly with the missiles attached. To fly the missiles, simply remove them again.

ATTACHING THE HARPOON TO THE GRIFFON

1.

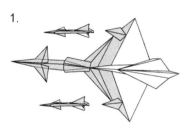

In order for the missiles to fit in the missile racks you must make a Griffon (see page 61) from a 7½ inch square and two harpoon missiles from two 2½ inch squares.

2.

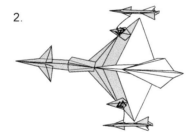

Take two perpendicular canard fins and slide them into the missile racks like shown.

3.

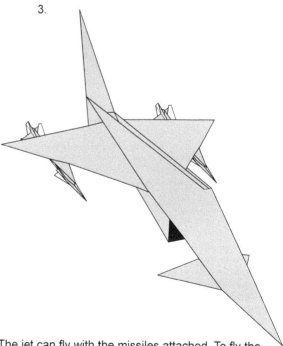

The jet can fly with the missiles attached. To fly the missiles, simply remove them again.

Use an 8½ x 8½ in. square sheet of paper.

1.
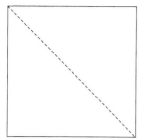

2.
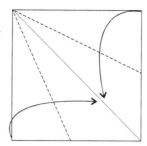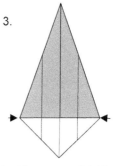

3.
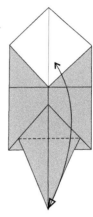

Inside reverse fold the
edges into the center.

4.
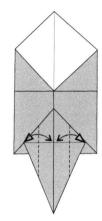

5.
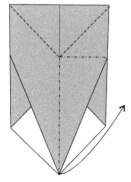

Rabbit ear fold the flap
as shown, then rotate
the paper 180°.

6.
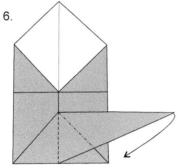

Squash fold the flap down.

7.

Fold the flap up, then
unfold.

8.

Fold the sides of the
flap in, then unfold.

9.

Fold the sides of the flap
along the creases you
just made, then unfold.

10.

Inside reverse fold
the sides in.

11.

Petal fold the flap up
using the creases you
made in step 9.

12.

13.

Pull the paper out from
underneath.

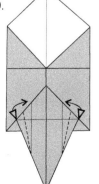
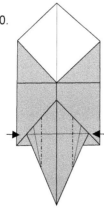
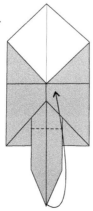
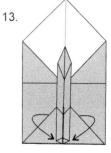

14.

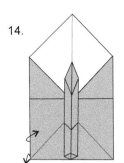

Take the top and bottom layers of the paper and gently pull them apart as shown in step 15.

15.

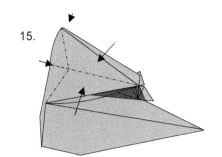

Push in along the lines and edges shown.

16.

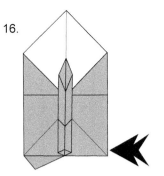

Repeat steps 14–15 on this side.

17.

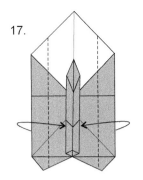

Fold the sides into the edges of the middle flap.

18.

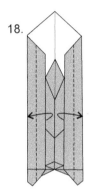

19.

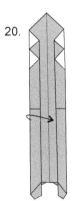

Fold the side behind. Fold the paper on the center flap behind, then turn the paper over.

20.

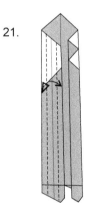

Fold the top layer over.

21.

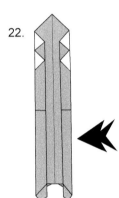

Add the valley folds and return the model to step 20.

22.

Repeat steps 20–21 on this side.

23.

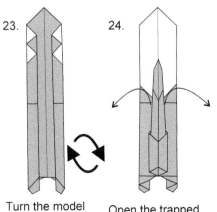

Turn the model over.

24.

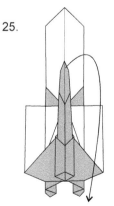

Open the trapped flaps out from underneath.

25.

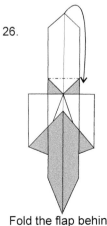

Unfold the flap to step 11.

26.

Fold the flap behind and turn the model over.

27.

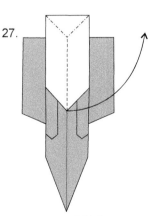

Rabbit ear fold the top flap.

28.

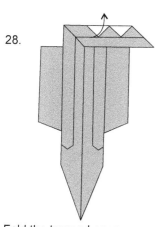

Fold the trapped paper up and repeat behind.

29.

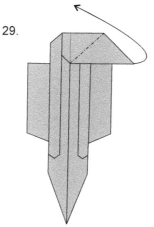

Squash fold the flap.

30.

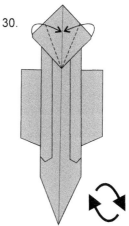

Fold the sides of the flap in, then turn the model over.

31.

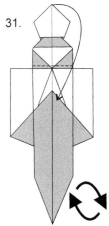

Fold the flap down under the layer shown as far as it will fit, then turn the model over.

32.

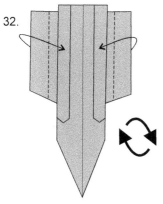

Fold the sides in as shown, then turn the model over.

33.

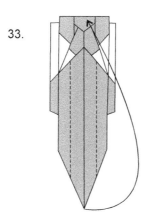

Return the flap to step 25.

34.

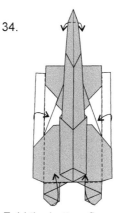

Fold the bottom flaps under the layers above, fold the sides in, and squash fold the tip of the top flap.

35.

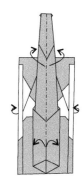

Rabbit ear fold the center flap so that it stands upright. Fold out the paper that is underneath the sides.

36.

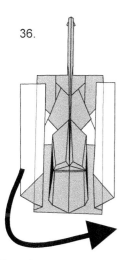

Turn the model so that the side is facing you.

37.

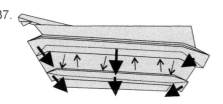

Pull the bottom layer of paper down while pushing the inner layer of paper to give the appearance of treads. Repeat behind.

38.

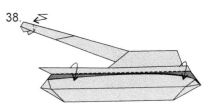

Fold the sides down, then repeat behind. Then crimp the barrel.

39.

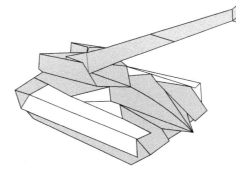

PREDATOR

MAIN BATTLE TANK

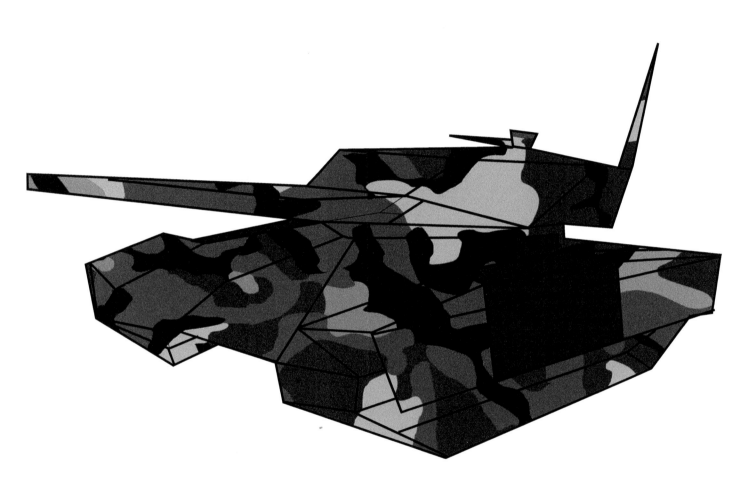

Use a 10 x 10 in. square of foil-backed paper.

1.

2.

3.

4.

Fold the sides in and swing the paper behind out.

5.

Rabbit ear fold the paper in on both sides. Then turn the model over.

6.

Fold the model in half, then turn it over.

7.

Petal fold the sides in using the existing creases.

8.

Swing the back flap up and fold the top flaps down. Then turn the model over.

9.

Petal fold the flap using the existing creases.

10.

Fold the top down and simultaneously fold the center flaps out.

11.

Fold the flaps up.

12.

Squash fold the center flap.

13.

Pull the side flaps down.

14.

Open sink the sides in.

15.

Fold the flaps facing you together, and fold the back in half. Then rotate the model 90°.

16.

Fold the top layer down and align the two corners shown.

17.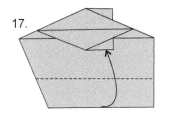

18.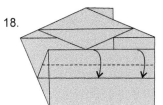

19.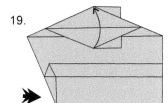

Repeat steps 17 and 18 on the other side.

20.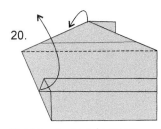

Fold the bottom layer up and the top back layer down.

21.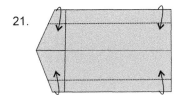

Using the edges underneath as a guide, fold the sides in.

22.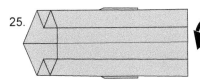

Fold the edge in.

23.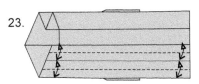

Fold and unfold using the center line.

24.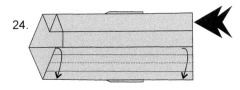

Fold the edge back down and repeat steps 22–24 on the other side.

25.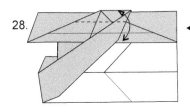

Turn the model over.

26.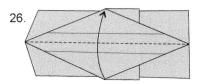

27.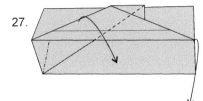

Squash fold the layer down.

28.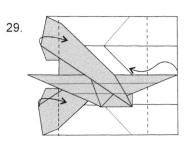

Fold then unfold the top layer. Then repeat steps 26–28 behind.

29.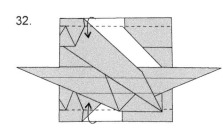

Fold the rear paper underneath. Fold the small flaps over.

30.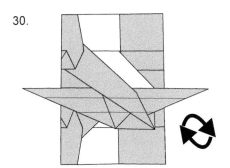

Turn the model over.

31.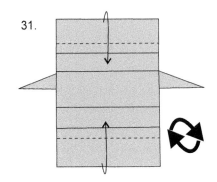

Fold the sides in, then turn the model over.

32.

33.

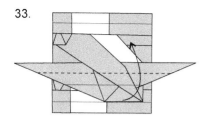

Fold the top flaps up on the existing creases so that they stand upright as shown in step 34.

34.

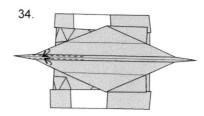

Pinch the front of the flap in half into the center line.

35.

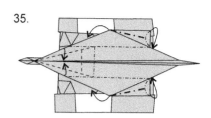

Shape the turret by first rolling the back edges in. Then fold the sides of the turret down. Finally, fold the sides of the barrel in.

36.

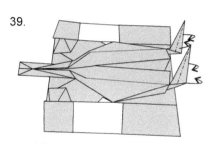

Squash fold the back flaps and reverse fold the tip of the barrel in.

37.

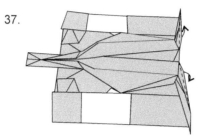

Valley fold the back edges in.

38.

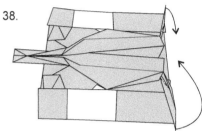

Inside reverse fold the two flaps in.

39.

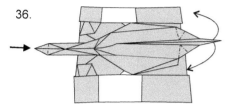

Mountain fold the sides in.

40.

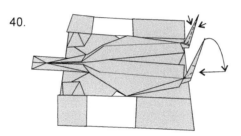

Pinch the antenna to narrow it. Then inside reverse fold the other flap twice to form a gun turret.

41.

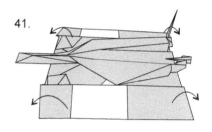

Bend the back and the front down. Then rotate the model around so the side is facing you.

42.

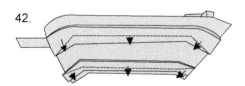

Using the preexisting creases pull the paper down to form tracks.

43.

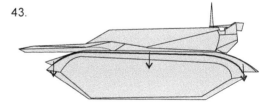

Fold the sides down along the preexisting creases.

44.

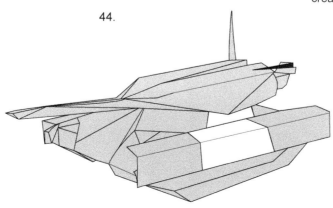

MARAUDER

ARMORED PERSONNEL CARRIER

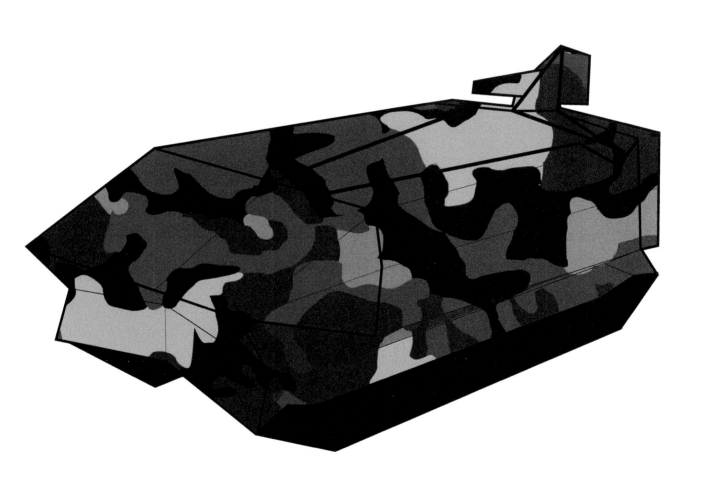

Use a 10 x 10 in. square sheet of foil paper.

1.
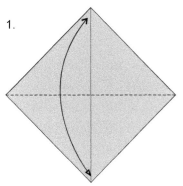
Begin with a preliminary fold.
Fold then unfold the top layer
only.

2.
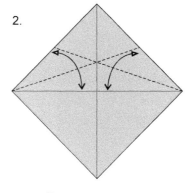
Fold then unfold.

3.
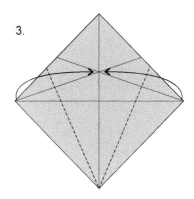

4.
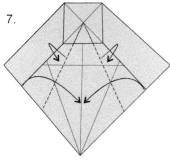
Fold the intersections noted down
to the edges.

5.
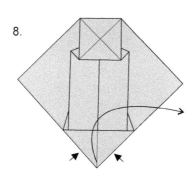
Squash fold the point down.

6.
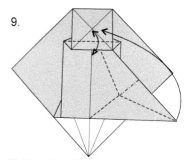
Mountain fold the sides in.

7.
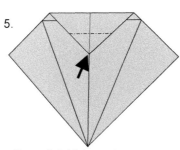
Fold the sides in while swinging
the hidden edges out.

8.
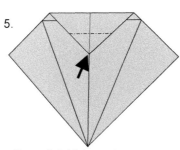
Pinch the bottom of the top layer
together and pull it to the side.

9.
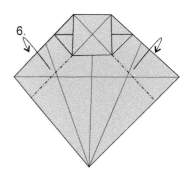
Fold and unfold the small area,
then rabbit ear fold the large flap
on the existing creases.

10.
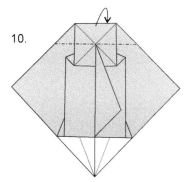
Mountain fold the paper behind
along existing creases.

11.
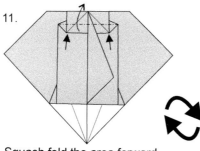
Squash fold the area forward,
then turn the model over.

12.
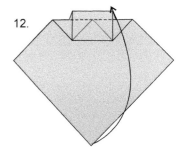
Petal fold the bottom flap up along
the crease shown.

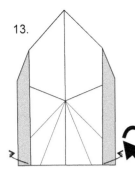
13.

Wrap the sides around, then turn the model over.

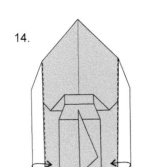
14.

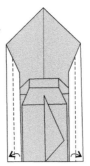
15.

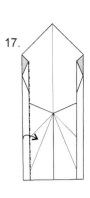
16.

Fold the edges behind, then turn the model over.

17.

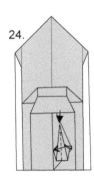
18.

Fold then unfold the small areas.

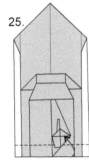
19.

Fold the side over and repeat step 18 on the other side.

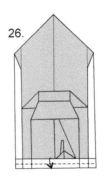
20.

Fold the sides out, then turn the model over.

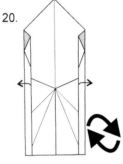
21.

Rabbit ear fold the flap down.

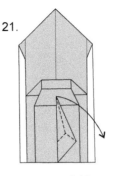
22.

Squash fold the flap down.

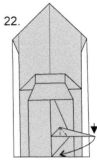
23.

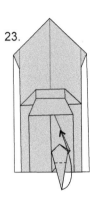
24.

Inside reverse fold the tip in, then fold the flap in half.

25.

26.

27.

Unfold the paper to step 25.

28.

Outside reverse fold the bottom edge along the line you just made.

29.

Swivel fold the paper down.

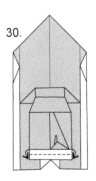
30.

Outside reverse fold the paper along the existing creases.

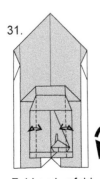
31.

Fold and unfold the sides in, then turn the model over.

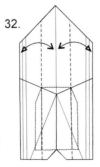
32.

Using the creases you just made behind, fold then unfold the sides.

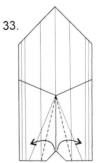
33.

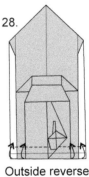
34.

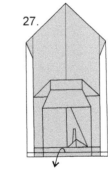
35.

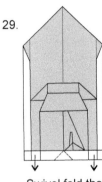
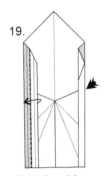
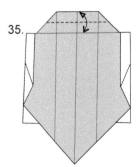

36.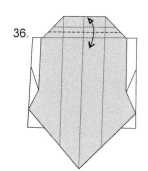

37.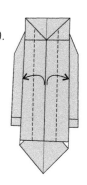

38.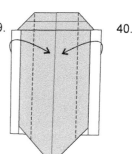

Using the crease you just made, shift the layer up so that it lies along the crease.

39.

40.

41.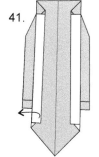

Bend back the top layer.

42.

Fold the corner in, then place the layer back down. Repeat on the other side.

43.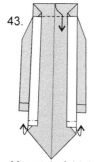

Mountain fold the small edges underneath. Valley fold the top edge underneath the tracks.

44.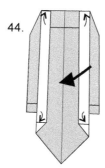

Curl the edges of the tracks in, then turn the model so the side is facing you.

45.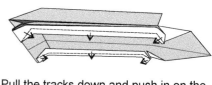

Pull the tracks down and push in on the existing creases.

46.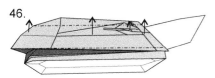

Fold the gun upright. Using the existing creases, pull up on the top layer and push the sides in.

47.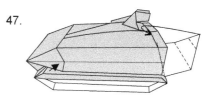

Push the sides in. Fold the ramp up and around so it locks into the pocket.

48.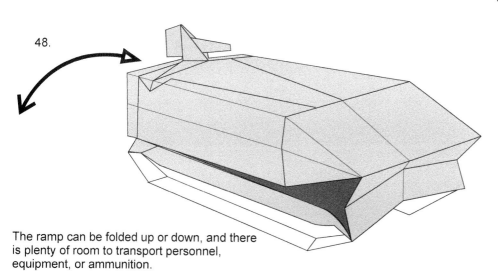

The ramp can be folded up or down, and there is plenty of room to transport personnel, equipment, or ammunition.

WARTHOG

ANTI-AIRCRAFT

Use a 10 x 10 in. square of foil backed paper.

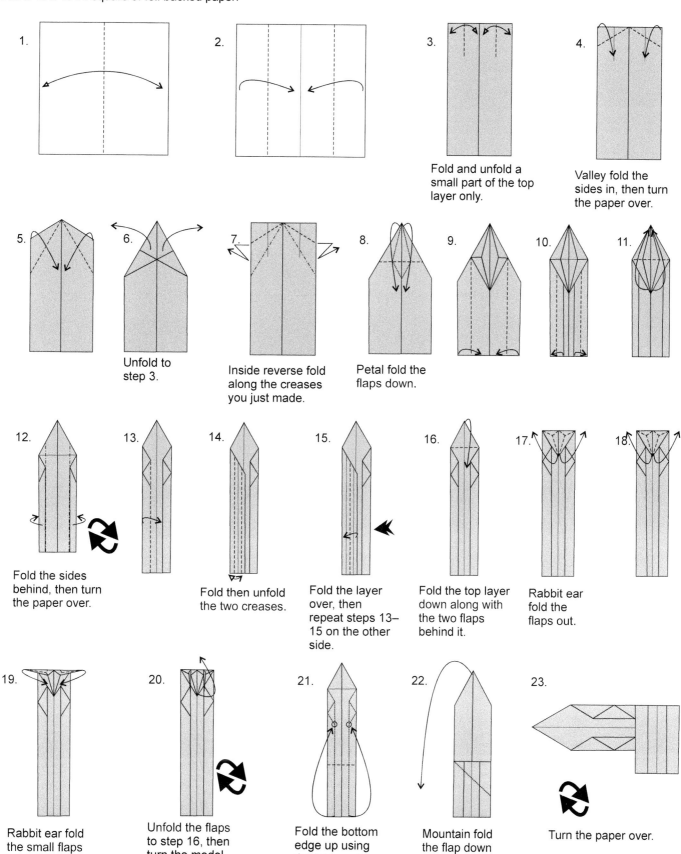

1.

2.

3.
Fold and unfold a small part of the top layer only.

4.
Valley fold the sides in, then turn the paper over.

5.

6.
Unfold to step 3.

7.
Inside reverse fold along the creases you just made.

8.
Petal fold the flaps down.

9.

10.

11.

12.
Fold the sides behind, then turn the paper over.

13.

14.
Fold then unfold the two creases.

15.
Fold the layer over, then repeat steps 13–15 on the other side.

16.
Fold the top layer down along with the two flaps behind it.

17.
Rabbit ear fold the flaps out.

18.

19.
Rabbit ear fold the small flaps up.

20.
Unfold the flaps to step 16, then turn the model over.

21.
Fold the bottom edge up using the intersection behind as a guide.

22.
Mountain fold the flap down using the same intersection as step 21.

23.
Turn the paper over.

24.

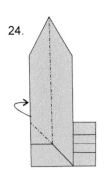

Rabbit ear fold the paper behind.

25.

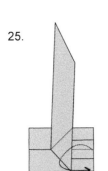

Pull out the paper underneath, and wrap it around the top layer.

26.

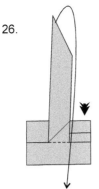

Fold the flap down, then repeat step 25 on the other side.

27.

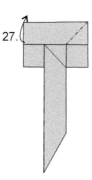

Squash fold the layer over.

28.

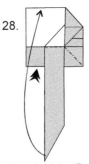

First fold the flap up, then repeat step 27 on the other side.

29.

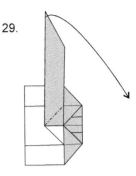

Squash fold the flap down.

30.

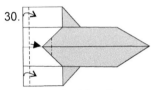

Open sink the triangle shown. Valley fold the edge in.

31.

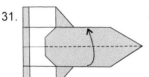

32.

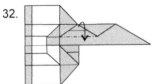

Fold the top pleat down.

33.

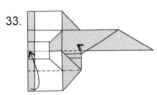

Valley fold the small excess paper up. Return the side to step 26.

34.

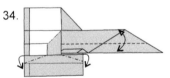

Fold then unfold the large flap in half. Fold the corners of the sides underneath the layers behind them.

35.

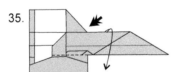

Fold both layers of the flap down and repeat steps 31–34 on the other side.

36.

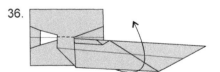

Valley fold both layers.

37.

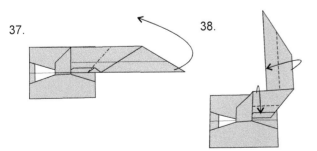

38.

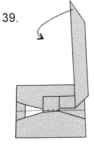

Swivel fold both sides of the flap in on the creases made in step 34.

39.

Fold the flap over so it stands upright.

40.

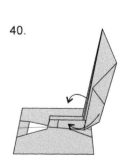

Fold the sides over

34

41.

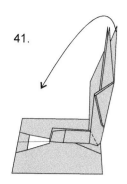

Fold the top of the flap down while folding the bottom out.

42.

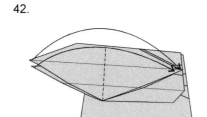

Fold all three flaps back.

43.

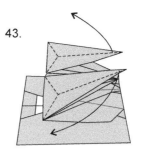

Rabbit ear fold the flaps down on the existing creases.

44.

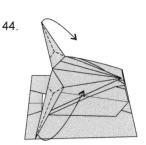

Partially rabbit ear fold the flaps down on the existing creases.

45.

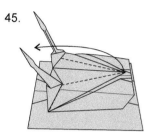

Fold the flap down while pushing the sides in. Part of the sides must fit underneath the narrow flaps.

46.

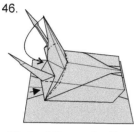

First roll the center flap under itself, then push all three flaps in together to form the front of the turret.

47.

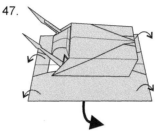

Roll the edges down, then turn model so the side faces you.

48.

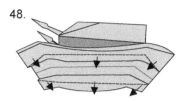

Pull the tracks down along the existing creases.

49.

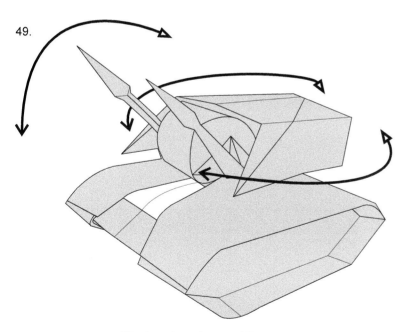

The turret can turn and the cannons can be raised and lowered up to 90°.

GUARDIAN
BATTLE WALKER

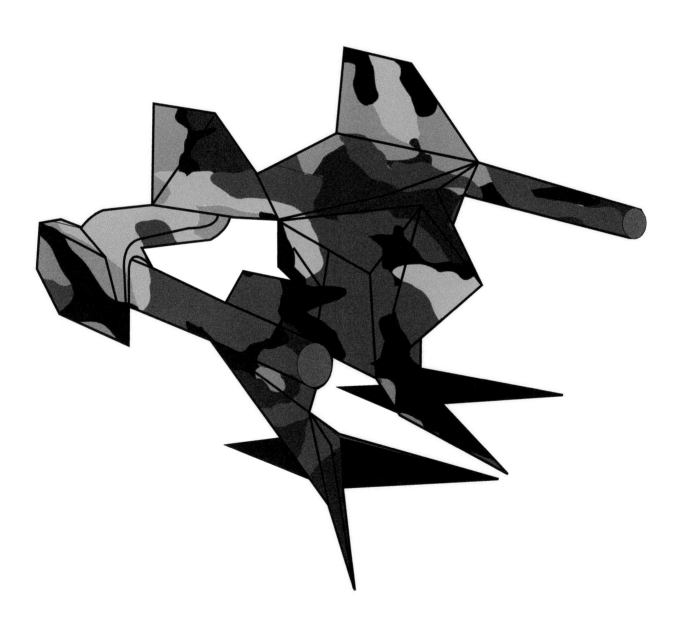

Use a 13 x 13 in. square sheet of foil paper

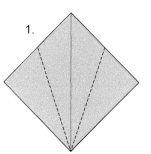
1.

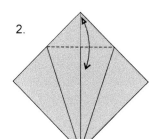
2.

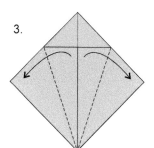
3.

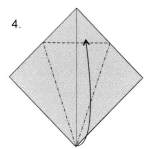
4.

Begin with a preliminary fold, and fold the sides in.

Petal fold the flap up.

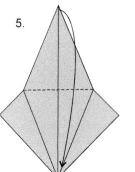
5.

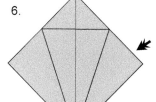
6.

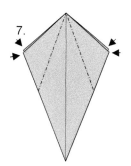
7.

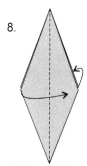
8.

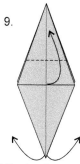
9.

Repeat steps 1–6 behind.

Squash fold the four corners in.

Fold one flap over in the front and one in the back.

Fold the top layer up as far as it will go and simultaneously swing the flaps out.

10.

11.

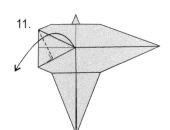
12.

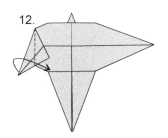
13.

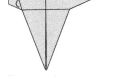

Fold the flap out perpendicular to its edge.

Fold the flap back to step 11.

14.

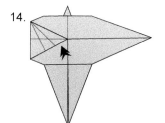
15.

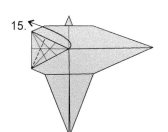
16.

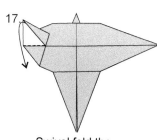
17.

Repeat steps 11–14 in the other direction.

Pull the trapped paper out from underneath.

Swivel fold the paper down.

18.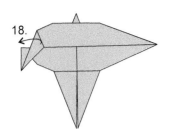

Pull the trapped paper out from underneath.

19.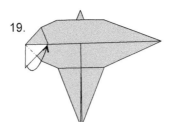

Outside reverse fold the paper up.

20.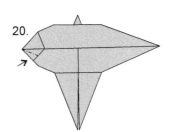

Inside reverse fold the small area.

21.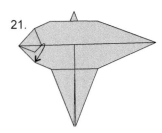

Pull the trapped paper out.

22.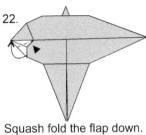

Squash fold the flap down.

23.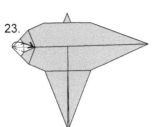

Petal fold the small flap over.

24.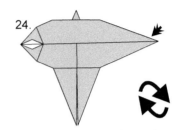

Repeat steps 10–24 on the other side, then turn the model over.

25.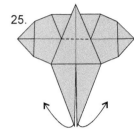

Fold the top layer up as far as it will go and simultaneously swing the flaps out.

26.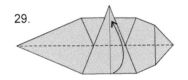

27.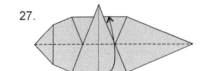

28.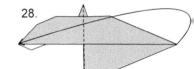

29.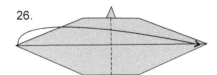

30.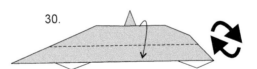

Fold the flap in half, then turn the paper over.

31.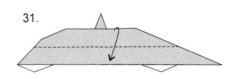

32.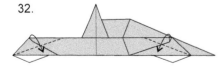

33.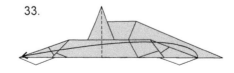

34.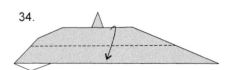

35.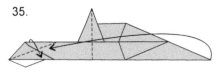

First fold the edge down, then fold the flap over.

36.

37.

38.

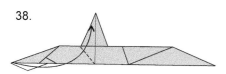

39.

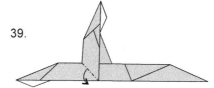

Pull the trapped paper out from underneath.

40.

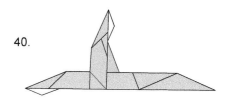

41.

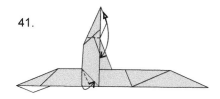

42.

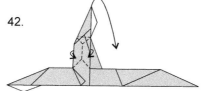

Perform a double rabbit ear fold on the flap.

43.

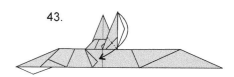

Inside reverse fold the flap over.

44.

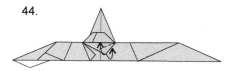

Fold the sides in front and back.

45.

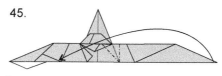

Swivel fold the flap down using the inside edge shown as a guide.

46.

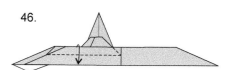

Swivel fold the edge down.

47.

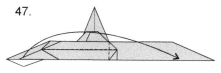

Swivel fold the flap back over.

48.

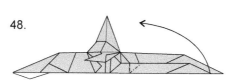

Squash fold the flap up using the edge behind as a guide.

49.

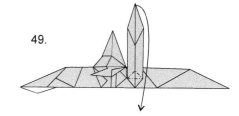

50.

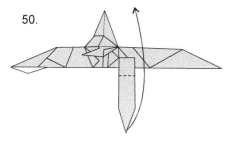

51.

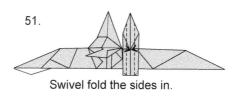

Swivel fold the sides in.

52.

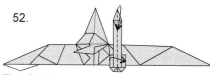

First fold the tip down, then fold the flap in half.

53.

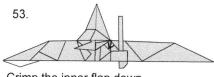

Crimp the inner flap down.

54.

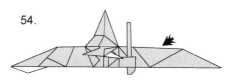

Repeat steps 38–54 behind.

55.

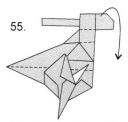

Position the model as shown in step 56 by folding the arms and legs out and the guns down.

56.

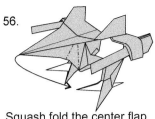

Squash fold the center flap down.

57.

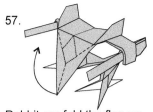

Rabbit ear fold the flap up. Note this will also form a petal fold behind.

58.

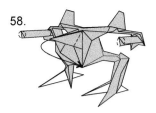

Round the guns. Outside reverse fold the center flap to form the cockpit.

59.

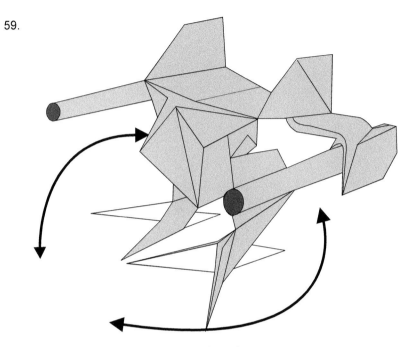

You can reposition the legs in various ways.

WRAITH

ELECTRONIC WARFARE

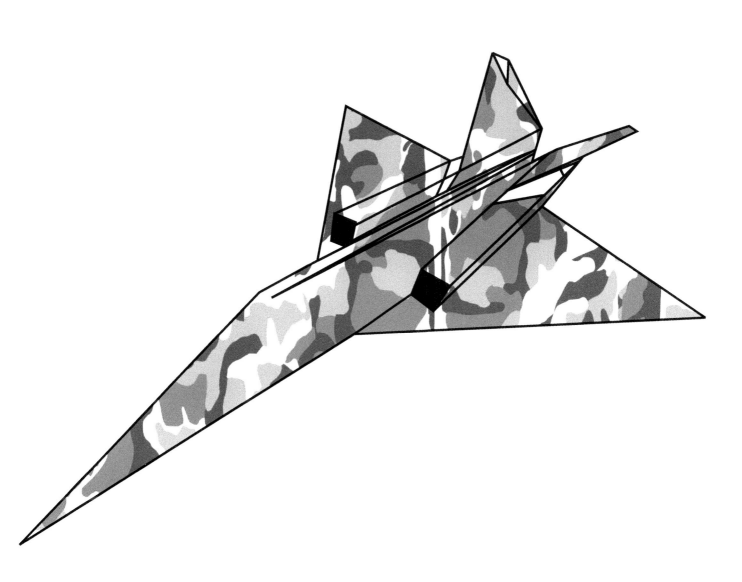

Use an 8½ x 8½ in. square sheet of paper.

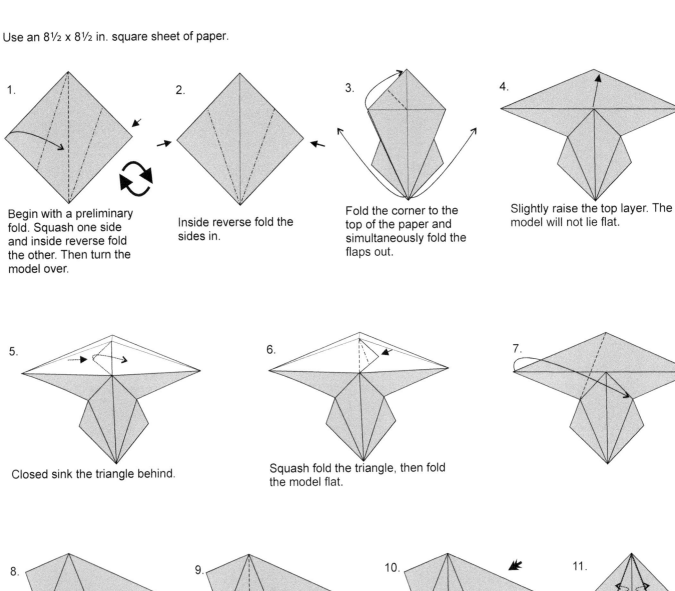

1.

Begin with a preliminary fold. Squash one side and inside reverse fold the other. Then turn the model over.

2.

Inside reverse fold the sides in.

3.

Fold the corner to the top of the paper and simultaneously fold the flaps out.

4.

Slightly raise the top layer. The model will not lie flat.

5.

Closed sink the triangle behind.

6.

Squash fold the triangle, then fold the model flat.

7.

8.

Pull the trapped paper out.

9.

10.

Repeat steps 6–10 on the other side.

11.

Pull the trapped paper out from underneath.

12.

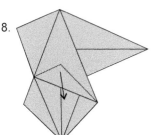

Inside petal fold the small area.

13.

14.

Squash fold the top area over.

15.

Pull the trapped paper out from underneath.

16.

17.

Repeat steps 13–17 on the other side.

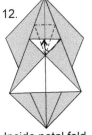 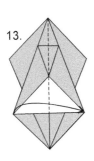 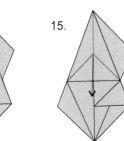 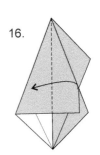 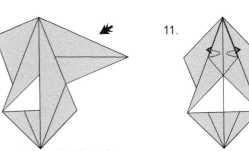 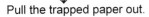 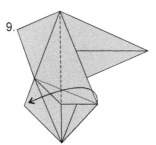

18.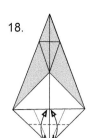

19.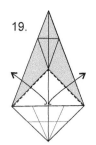

20.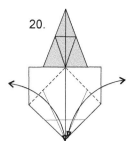

21.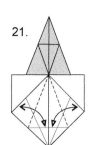

22.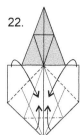

Outside reverse fold the tips of the flaps up. Then fold the upper flaps down.

23.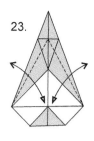

24.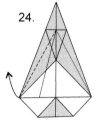

Swivel fold the flap up.

25.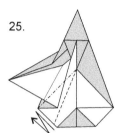

Inside reverse fold the flap along the existing creases.

26.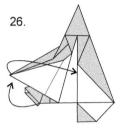

Fold the flap over and swing the lower area up. Refer to step 27.

27.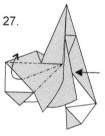

Continue to swivel fold the paper up and fold the flap flat.

28.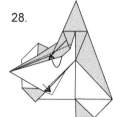

Pull the paper out from underneath. Fold the paper on the large flap in.

29.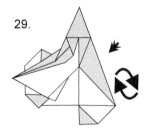

Repeat steps 24–28 on the other side. Then turn the model over.

30.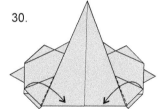

31.

Fold the flaps into the pockets.

32.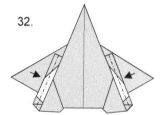

Squash fold these areas over.

33.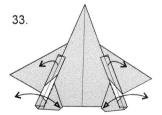

First fold then unfold the tailfins. Fold the rectangular areas back to step 32. Then turn the model over.

34.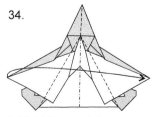

Jet fold the model as shown.

35.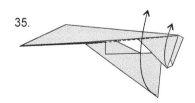

36.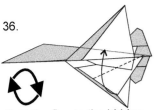

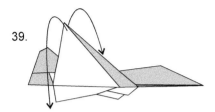

Fold the flap to the hidden edge shown. Then turn the model over.

37.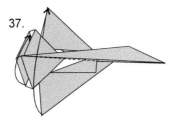

38.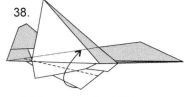

Fold the flap to the hidden edge shown.

39.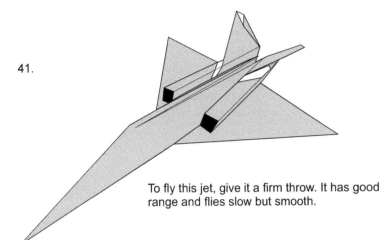

Fold the wings down.

40.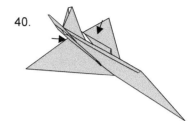

Reform the squash folds you made in step 33. Then fold the tailfins down.

41.

To fly this jet, give it a firm throw. It has good range and flies slow but smooth.

SPECTRE

SPY PLANE

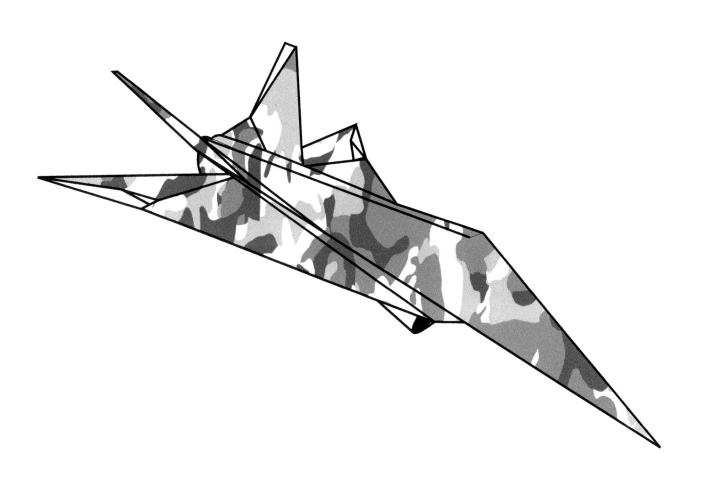

Use an 8½ x 8½ in. square sheet of paper.

1.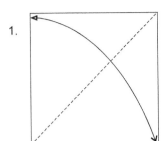

2.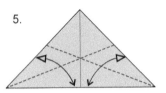

3.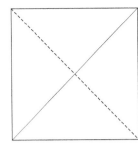

4.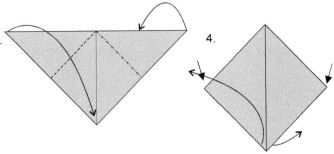

Open the bottom layers and push the sides in. This will form a water bomb base.

5.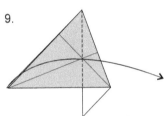

6.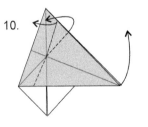

Fold the flap over and push the bottom up.

7.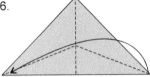

Fold then unfold.

8.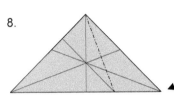

Inside reverse fold the flap in.

9.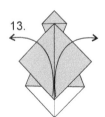

Fold both flaps over and repeat steps 7 and 8 on the other side.

10.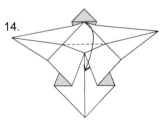

11.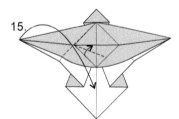

Continue to flatten the paper.

12.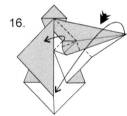

13.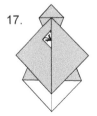

Fold the flaps so that they stand upright.

14.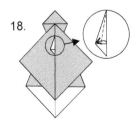

Fold the middle layer of paper down.

15.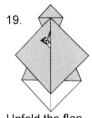

Fold the center layer over and push the flap over it.

16.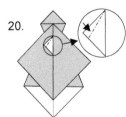

Repeat step 15 on the other side.

17.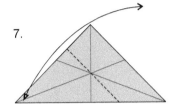

18.

19.

Unfold the flap to step 17.

20.

Inside reverse fold the small area using the crease you made in step 19.

21.

Fold the flaps out.

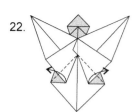

22.

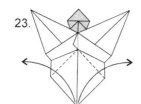

23.

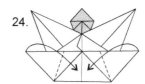

24.

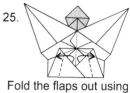

25.
Fold the flaps out using the edge underneath as a guide.

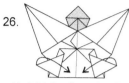

26.
Unfold the flaps back to step 25.

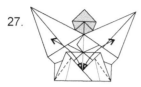

27.
Fold the flaps up, then unfold.

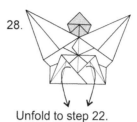

28.
Unfold to step 22.

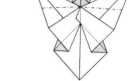

29.
Squash fold the flaps in half.

30.
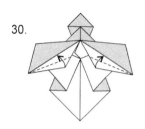

31.
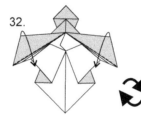
Mountain fold the sides of the flaps to the inner edge shown.

32.
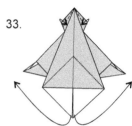
Fold the flaps down, then turn the model over.

33.
Fold the small edges in. Inside reverse fold the bottom flaps out using the existing creases.

34.
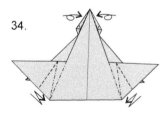
Fold the small area over twice into the model. Inside reverse fold the bottom flaps along the existing creases.

35.
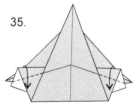
Fold the flaps down. You will have to partially fold them inside.

36.
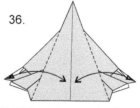
Fold the wings and tail fins in, then unfold. Then turn the model over.

37.
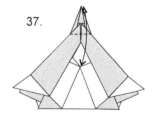

38.
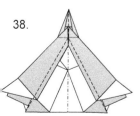
Jet fold the model using the crease you just made as a guide.

39.
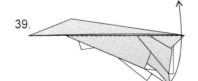
Fold the wings, tailfins, and the two layers behind up.

40.
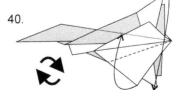
Fold the flap into the hidden edge shown. Fold the wings and tailfin down. Then turn the model over.

41.
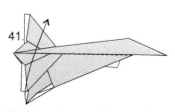
Fold the wings, tailfins, and the two layers behind up.

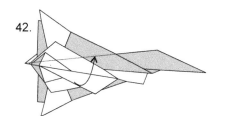

42.

Fold the flap into the hidden edge shown.

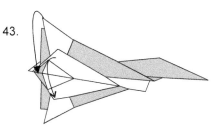

43.

Fold the inner layers down. Fold the wings down. Fold the tailfins out and turn the model so the bottom faces you.

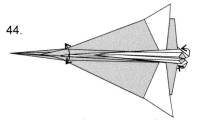

44.

Roll the rear flaps over each other into a round shape to form an afterburner. Round the small flap at the front to form an air intake.

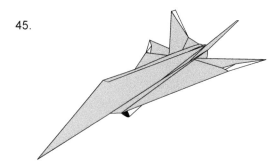

45.

Once properly balanced, this jet can fly up to 90 feet.

VIPER
INTERCEPTOR

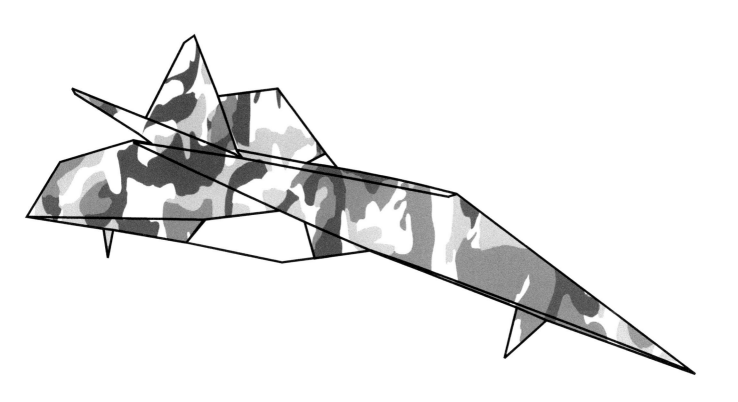

Use an 8½ x 8½ in. square sheet of paper.

1.
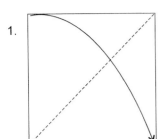

2.
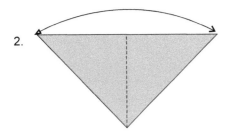

3.
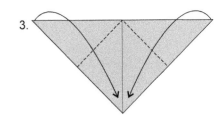

4.
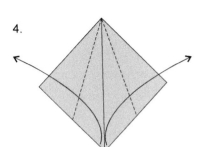

5.
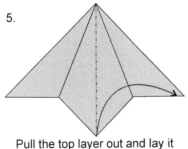

Pull the top layer out and lay it over.

6.
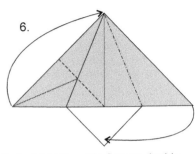

Swivel fold the side flap up. Inside reverse fold the flap you just made in.

7.
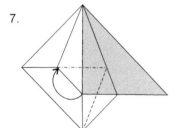

Inside petal fold the flap in.

8.
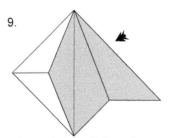

Fold both layers over.

9.
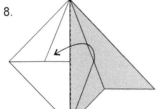

Repeat steps 6–8 on the other side.

10.
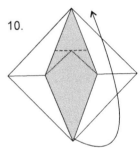

Swivel fold the top flap up as far as it will go.

11.
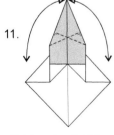

Fold and unfold the flap perpendicular to its edge.

12.
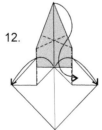

Open the sides of the flap out. Fold the top part down and over using existing creases.

13.
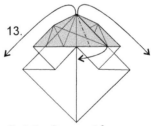

Pull the flaps out from underneath. Squash fold the small center flap.

14.
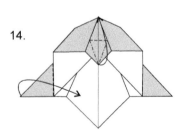

Petal fold the flap up. Fold the lower flap over.

15.
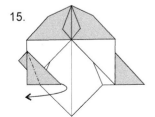

Squash fold the flap.

16.
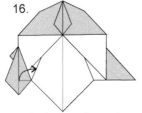

Pull the inner edge out.

17.
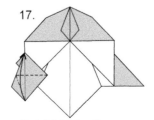

Petal fold the flap up.

18.
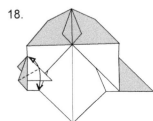

Fold the layer down, then unfold it.

19.

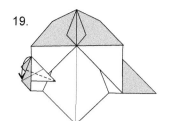

20.

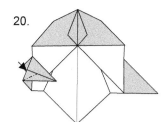

Inside reverse fold the small
flap using the crease you
just made.

21.

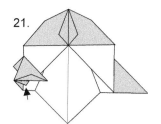

Inside reverse fold the
small area up.

22.

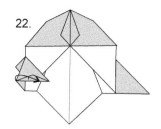

23.

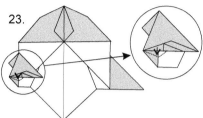

Pull the small layer out.

24.

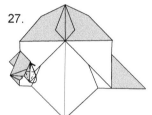

Pull the small layer out.

25.

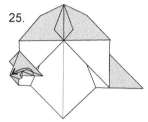

Fold the small flap over.

26.

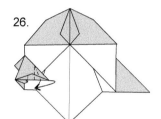

Squash fold the flap down.

27.

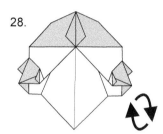

Petal fold the flap up. Repeat
steps 14–27 on the other side.

28.

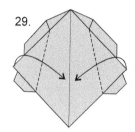

Turn the model over.

29.

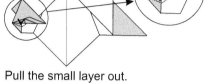

30.

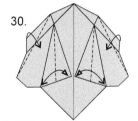

Fold the outer edges in as
shown. Fold the inner
edges in, then unfold
them.

31.

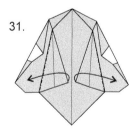

32.

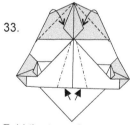

Inside reverse fold the
sides in, then turn the
model over.

33.

Fold the top edges
down. Inside reverse fold
the inner edges along
the existing crease.

34.

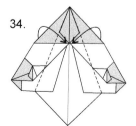

35.

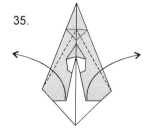

Fold the flaps out using
the intersection
underneath as a guide.

36.

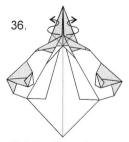

Pull the inner flap out
and place it on the
layers above it.

37.

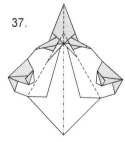

Jet fold the model
using the inner edges
of the wings as a
guide.

38.

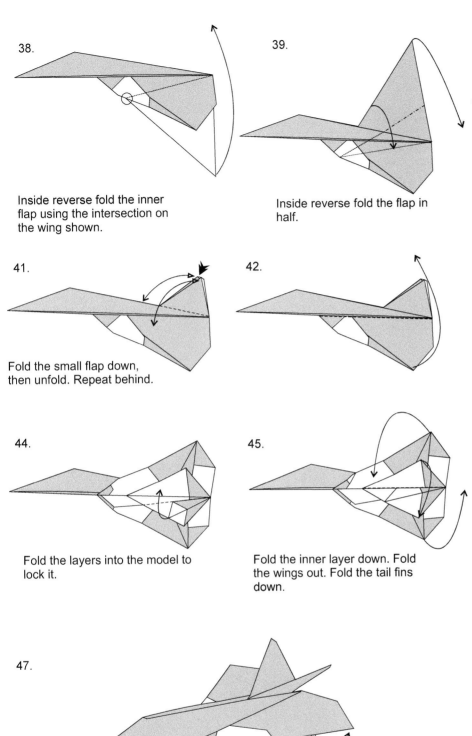

Inside reverse fold the inner
flap using the intersection on
the wing shown.

39.

Inside reverse fold the flap in
half.

40.

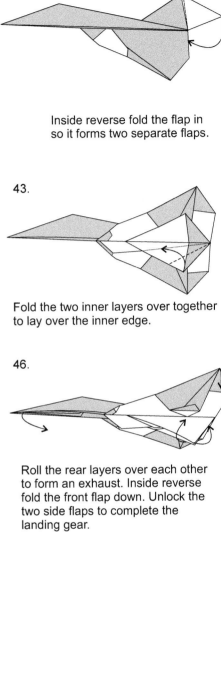

Inside reverse fold the flap in
so it forms two separate flaps.

41.

Fold the small flap down,
then unfold. Repeat behind.

42.

43.

Fold the two inner layers over together
to lay over the inner edge.

44.

Fold the layers into the model to
lock it.

45.

Fold the inner layer down. Fold
the wings out. Fold the tail fins
down.

46.

Roll the rear layers over each other
to form an exhaust. Inside reverse
fold the front flap down. Unlock the
two side flaps to complete the
landing gear.

47.

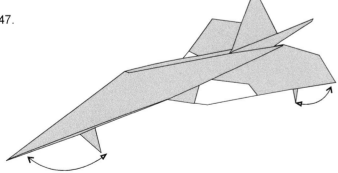

To fly this plane, fold up the landing gear, then grab the
keel and give it a hard throw. It is capable of flying up to
70 feet.

FALCON
STRIKE FIGHTER

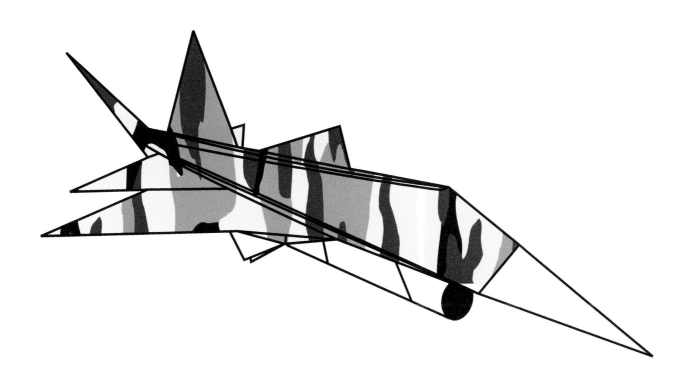

Use an 8½ x 8½ in. square sheet of paper.

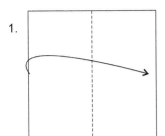

1.

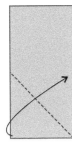

2.

3.

Squash fold the flap.

4.

Turn the model over.

5.

Squash fold the top of the model.

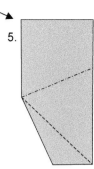

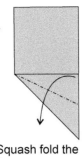

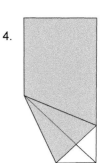

6.

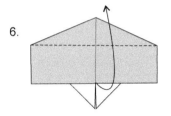

7.

Turn the model over.

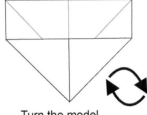

8.

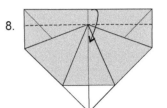

9.

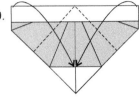

10.

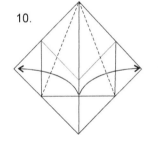

11.

Turn the model over.

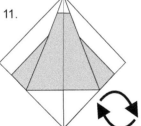

12.

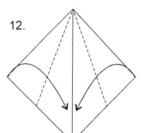

13.

Pull the paper out from underneath.

14.

Petal fold the top flap. Fold the bottom layers out.

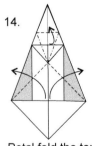

15.

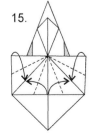

16.

17.

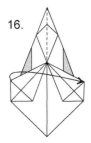

18.

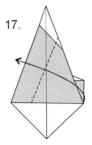

19.

Fold the layer out from underneath.

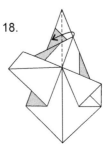

20.

Fold the layer out from underneath.

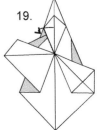

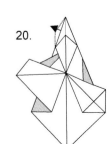

21.

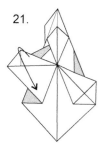

Pull the trapped paper down as far as it will go.

22.

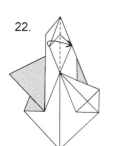

23.

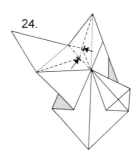

Pull the top layer of paper up. The paper will not lie flat.

24.

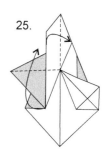

Push in on the areas shown, and use the existing crease to lay the model flat.

25.

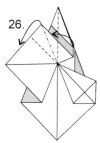

Swivel fold the paper over.

26.

Swivel fold the paper over.

27.

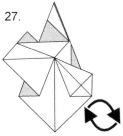

Turn the model over.

28.

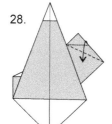

Swivel fold the paper down.

29.

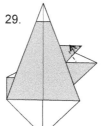

Swivel fold the small area up.

30.

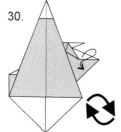

Fold the top layer into the pocket underneath, then turn the model over.

31.

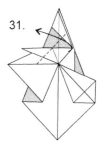

Fold the flap over as far as it will go.

32.

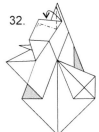

Swivel fold the area behind. The fold must be perpendicular to its edge.

33.

Swivel fold the paper down.

34.

35.

Fold the edge of the triangle to the edge shown then unfold.

36.

37.

Unfold the flap to step 32.

38.

Inside reverse fold along the creases you just made.

39.

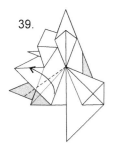

40.

Push the paper down.

41.

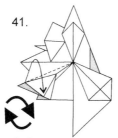

Pull the layer down and pull the excess paper behind it. Then turn the model over.

42.

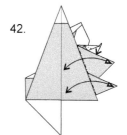

Fold then unfold the wings and tailfins only. Inside reverse fold the small flap in, then turn the model over.

43.

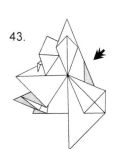

Repeat steps 16–41 on the other side.

44.

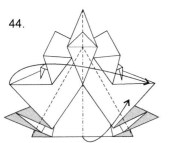

Jet fold the model as shown.

45.

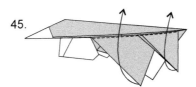

Fold the wings and tailfins up.

46.

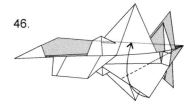

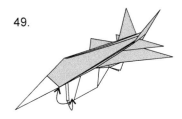

Fold the flap into the hidden edge shown. Then turn the model over.

47.

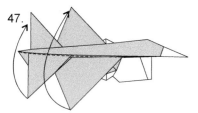

Fold the wings and tailfins up.

48.

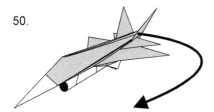

Fold the flap into the hidden edge shown. Then turn the model so that the front is facing you.

49.

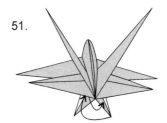

Roll one of the flaps into the pocket of the other. This will form an air intake.

50.

Turn the model so that the back is facing you.

51.

Roll one of the flaps over the other to form an afterburner.

52.

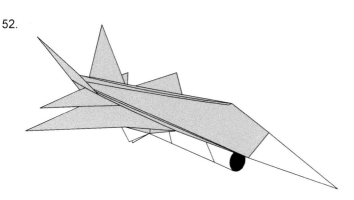

To fly this plane, give it a moderate throw. It has a range of 50 to 60 feet and good manueverability.

BRIMSTONE

BOMBER

Use a 13 x 13 in. square of foil paper

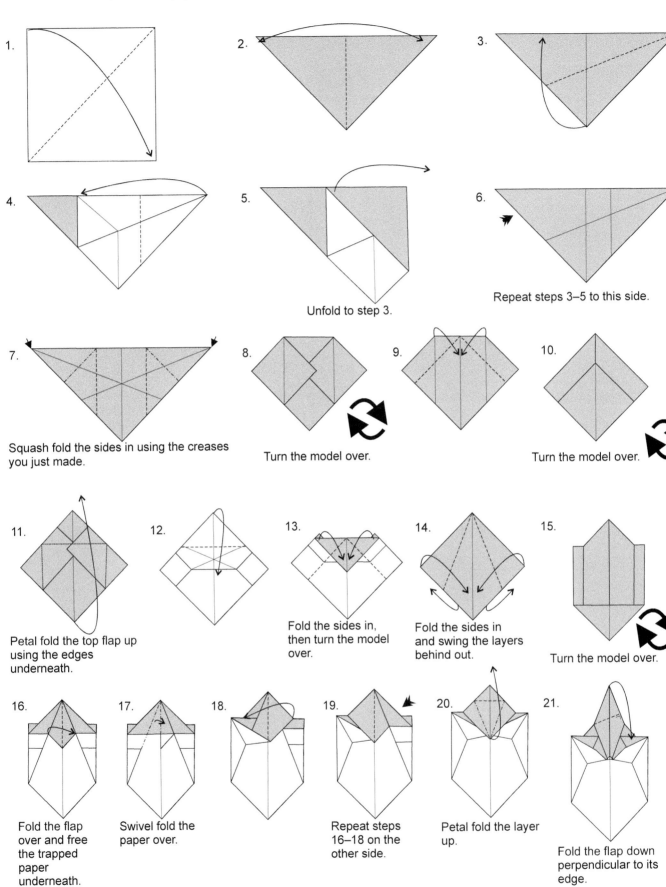

1.

2.

3.

4.

5.

Unfold to step 3.

6.

Repeat steps 3–5 to this side.

7.

Squash fold the sides in using the creases you just made.

8.

Turn the model over.

9.

10.

Turn the model over.

11.

Petal fold the top flap up using the edges underneath.

12.

13.

Fold the sides in, then turn the model over.

14.

Fold the sides in and swing the layers behind out.

15.

Turn the model over.

16.

Fold the flap over and free the trapped paper underneath.

17.

Swivel fold the paper over.

18.

19.

Repeat steps 16–18 on the other side.

20.

Petal fold the layer up.

21.

Fold the flap down perpendicular to its edge.

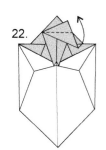
22.

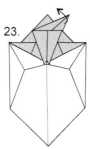
23.

Unfold the flap to step 21.

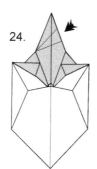
24.

Repeat steps 21–23 on the other side.

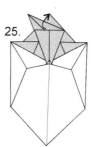
25.

Pull the trapped paper out from underneath.

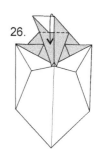
26.
27.

Swivel fold the paper over.

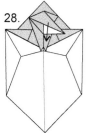
28.

Pull the paper out from underneath.

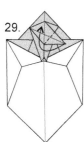
29.

Fold the paper underneath.

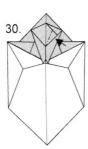
30.

Inside reverse fold the small flap in.

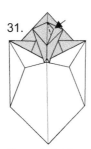
31.
32.

Squash fold the small area.

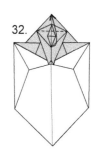
33.

Swivel fold the flaps down.

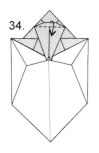
34.

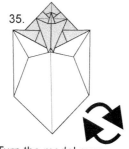
35.

Turn the model over.

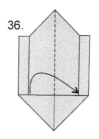
36.

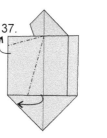
37.

Swivel the layer over so it is perpendicular to the edge underneath. Refer to step 38.

38.

Lay the flap down along with the rest of the paper.

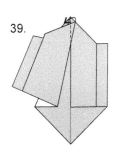
39.

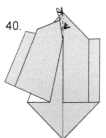
40.

Fold the small area over, then fold the excess paper in.

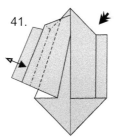
41.

Squash fold the side in then unfold it. Then repeat steps 36–41 on the other side.

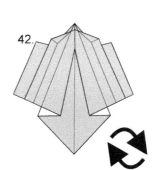
42.

Turn the model over.

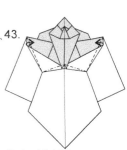
43.

Swivel fold the paper over to reposition it.

44.

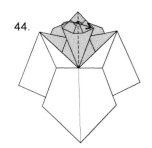

45.

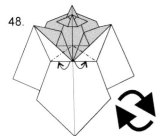

Swivel fold the paper over.

46.

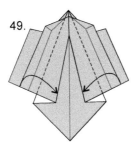

47.

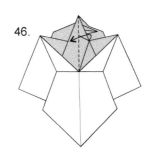

Repeat steps 44–46 on the other side.

48.

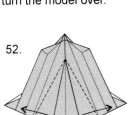

Fold the paper into the pocket underneath, then turn the model over.

49.

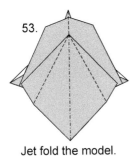

50.

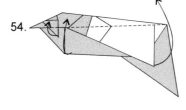

Fold the sides in.

51.

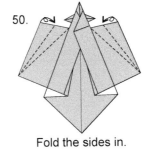

52.

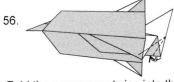

53.

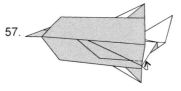

Jet fold the model.

54.

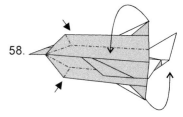

55.

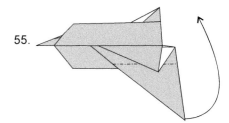

56.

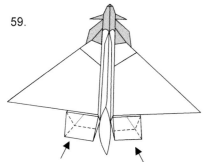

Fold the paper over twice into the model.

57.

Fold the excess paper in on both sides.

58.

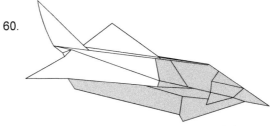

Squash fold the bomb bays out, then fold the wings and canard wings down. Rotate the model so the back is facing you.

59.

Fold in the back of the bomb bays, if you wish to place anything inside you can just reverse the folds.

60.

To fly this jet, grab the edge below the bomb bays and throw with moderate force. To deploy the bombs simply open the back and throw. The jet should fly up to 60 feet with or without a payload. The missiles will fit inside the bomb bays.

GRIFFON
AIR SUPERIORITY

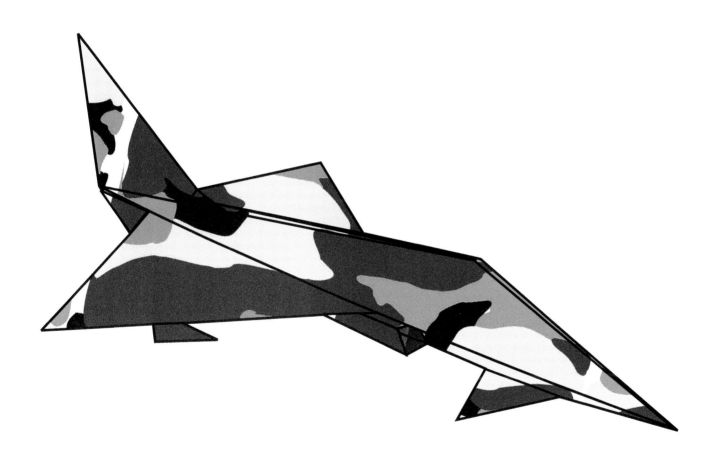

Use a 7½ x 7½ in. square piece of paper.

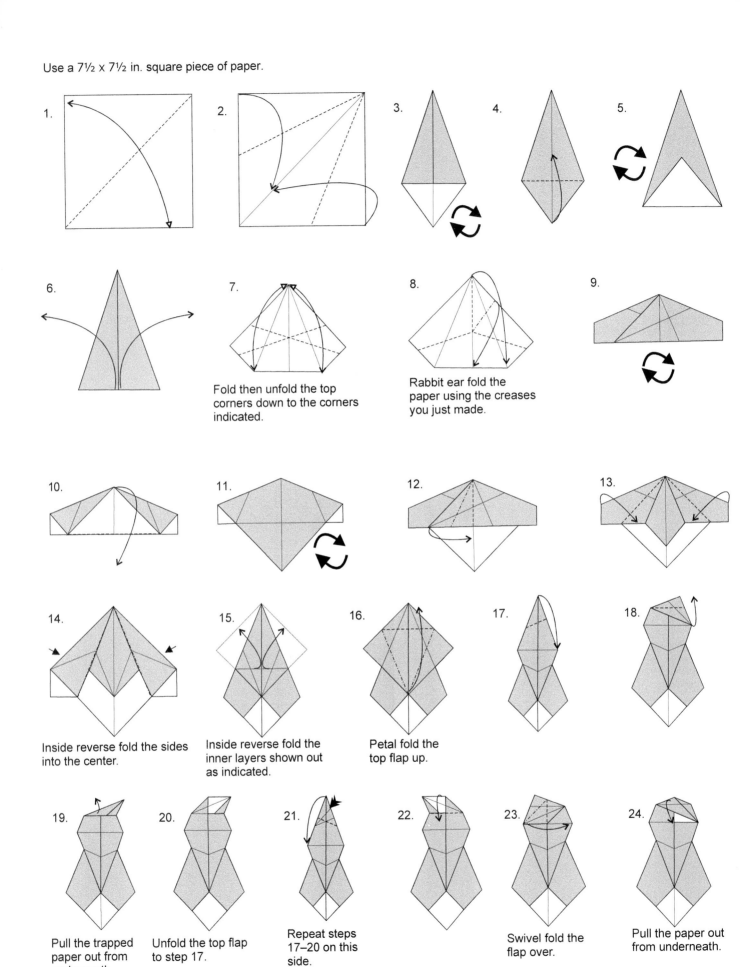

7. Fold then unfold the top corners down to the corners indicated.

8. Rabbit ear fold the paper using the creases you just made.

14. Inside reverse fold the sides into the center.

15. Inside reverse fold the inner layers shown out as indicated.

16. Petal fold the top flap up.

19. Pull the trapped paper out from underneath.

20. Unfold the top flap to step 17.

21. Repeat steps 17–20 on this side.

23. Swivel fold the flap over.

24. Pull the paper out from underneath.

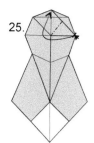
25. Inside reverse fold the flap in.

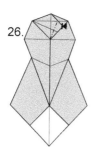
26. Inside reverse fold the paper in.

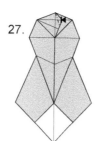
27. Squash fold the paper.

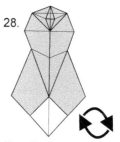
28. Turn the paper over.

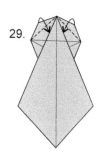
29.

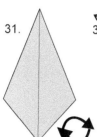
30. Fold the sides underneath the top layer.

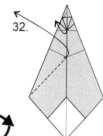
31. Turn the paper over.

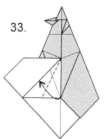
32. Inside reverse fold the top flap out, then valley fold the bottom flap over.

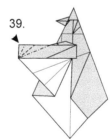
33.

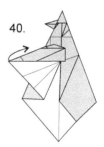
34. Swivel fold the flap up using the fold you just made.

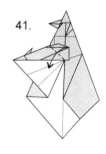
35. Valley fold the flap over.

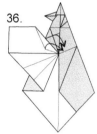
36. Pull out the trapped paper as shown.

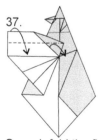
37. Squash fold the flap down.

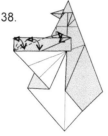
38. Swivel fold then unfold the area shown, then valley fold and unfold the flap as shown.

39. Inside reverse fold the flap in and out using the creases you made.

40. Inside reverse fold the flap up as shown.

41.

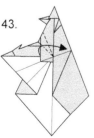
42. Fold the paper underneath along the crease you made in step 39.

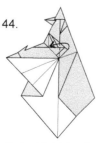
43. Swivel fold the flap over on the creases.

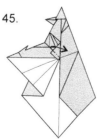
44. Swivel fold the flap as shown.

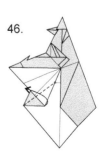
45. Unfold the flap back to step 44.

46.

47. Fold the flap underneath using the crease.

48.

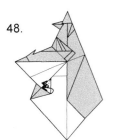

Squash fold the small flap.

49.

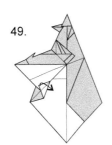

Unfold the flap to step 48.

50.

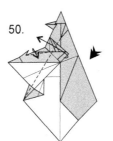

Fold the flap over as shown and repeat steps 32–50 on the other side.

51.

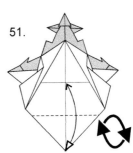

Fold the flap up to the lines shown, then unfold. Turn the model over.

52.

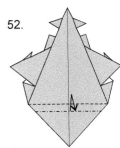

Fold the bottom flap along the lines shown.

53.

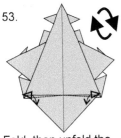

Fold, then unfold the flap as shown.

54.

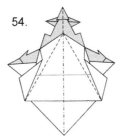

Jet fold the model.

55.

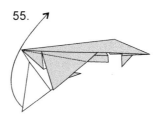

Inside reverse fold the flap up.

56.

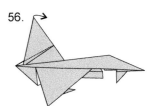

Using the creases you made in step 54, pull the flap forward.

57.

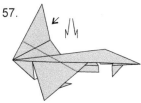

Carefully crimp the flap downwards as shown in step 59.

58.

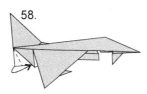

Fold all layers together to the edge shown.

59.

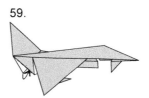

Fold the paper underneath the edge shown.

60.

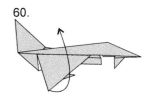

61.

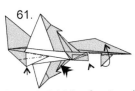

Squash fold the front and rear areas as shown and fold the small flap in the front up. Repeat behind.

62.

Fold the wings and canard wings down. Fold the missile racks out. Open out the afterburners and the air intakes.

63.

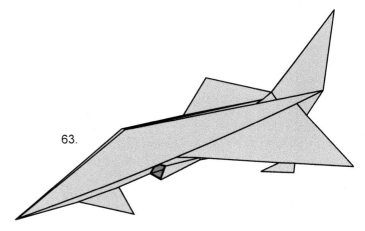

Give the jet a firm throw. It has good range and maneuverability.